FORT MOSE

FORT MOSE

COLONIAL AMERICA'S BLACK FORTRESS OF
FREEDOM

Kathleen Deagan and Darcie MacMahon

University Press of Florida / Florida Museum of Natural History

Acknowledgments

This publication has been financed in part with historic preservation grant assistance provided by the Bureau of Historic Preservation, Division of Historical Resources, Florida Department of State, assisted by the Historic Preservation Advisory Council. However, the contents and opinions do not necessarily reflect the views and opinions of the Florida Department of State, nor does the mention of trade names or commercial products constitute endorsement or recommendation by the Florida Department of State.

Florida Museum of Natural History Team:
Kathleen Deagan, Principal Investigator and Exhibit Curator
Darcie MacMahon, Exhibit Coordinator and Assistant Curator
Dort Dennis, Exhibit Designer and Production Coordinator
Betty Camp, Education Curriculum Material Development

Historical and Exhibit Consultants:
Jane Landers, Vanderbilt University
Theresa Singleton, Smithsonian Institution
Peter Wood, Duke University
Robin Poynor, University of Florida
Luis Arana, National Park Service
Albert Manucy, Architectural Historian

Educational and Exhibit Consultants:
Sterlin Adams, Florida A & M University
Representative Bill Clark, Florida Legislature
Cynthia Mingo, Prairie View Elementary
Joseph Taylor, Bethune Cookman College
Linda Woodcock, Glen Springs Elementary

Video Consultant:
Suellyn Winkle, Executive Producer

Exhibit Design and Construction:
Presentations South, Inc.
Florida Screen Services, Inc.

Brochure and Book Design:
Kelly Russ, Landers Design
Jim Landers, Landers Design
Vickie Kersey, Florida Museum of Natural History

Exhibit Artists:
Graphic Art: Stacey Breheny, Michael Falck, Presentations South
Models: Bob Leavy, Ron Chesser, Jay Weber
Photography: Stan Blomeley, James Quine, Pat Payne, Kathleen Deagan, University of Florida Office of Instructional Resources

Fort Mose Site Locator and Property Owner, 1968–1990:
F.E. "Jack" Williams, St. Augustine

Exhibition Funding Provided By:
The Florida Legislature
The Jessie Ball duPont Religious, Charitable and Educational Fund
The Florida Humanities Council (formerly the Florida Endowment for the Humanities)
The Florida Department of State, Bureau of Historical Museums
Florida Museum of Natural History

The University Press of Florida is the scholarly publishing agency for the State University System of Florida, comprised of Florida A & M University, Florida Atlantic University, Florida International University, Florida State University, University of Central Florida, University of Florida, University of North Florida, University of South Florida, and University of West Florida.

University Press of Florida
15 Northwest 15th Street
Gainesville, FL 32611
http://www.upf.com

CONTENTS

PREFACE

More than 250 years ago, African-born slaves risked their lives to escape from forced labor on English plantations in South Carolina. Hearing that the Spaniards in Florida promised religious sanctuary to runaway slaves, they made their way south to St. Augustine. In 1738, when more than 100 African fugitives had arrived in St. Augustine, the Spanish established the fort and town of Gracia Real de Santa Teresa de Mose, the first legally-sanctioned free black town in what is now the United States..

This is the story of Fort Mose and the people who lived there. It begins in Africa, and traces the roots of this eighteenth century free black town through Iberia and Spanish America to the colonial southeastern United States. It is also the story of how archaeologists, historians, space scientists, teachers and politicians worked together to bring the rich but neglected history of African Americans in the Spanish colonies to the North American public.

The site of Fort Mose has been the focus of a multidisciplinary historical archaeological research program since 1986, carried out by the Florida Museum of Natural History and funded by the State of Florida. Although the site was located in 1976 by its then-owner Jack Williams of St. Augustine, it was not until 1985 that efforts to secure funding for the study of the Mose site were successful. In that year Florida State Representative Bill Clark of Ft. Lauderdale visited the site, and was both moved and impressed by its importance to African-American history. Clark introduced a bill to the Florida legislature that provided funds for the historical and scientific study of Fort Mose. That work began in 1986 under Principal Investigator Kathleen Deagan.

The first six months of the project were devoted to documentary research in Spain and Florida by Historian Jane Landers, followed by two years of intensive archaeological field and laboratory research. Two more years were spent at the Florida Museum of Natural History developing a traveling exhibit, *Fort Mose: America's Black Fortress of Freedom*, that opened in 1991.

This volume is intended as a tribute to the ancestors of American people of African heritage. The rich diversity and multiple facets of this heritage are only poorly understood by most Americans today. Although slavery was the dominant theme, this part of their story is about the relentless pursuit of freedom, and the courage and vision to make effective choices toward self-determination when no choices seemed possible.

SPANISH SANCTUARY

In the turbulent frontier society of eighteenth century colonial southeastern North America, African slaves created opportunities to gain their freedom, taking advantage of the conflicts among the Spaniards, the English and the American Indians. With Indian allies they escaped from English plantations and made their way to Spanish Florida.

Spain and England, the two European powers who settled most of North America's southeastern region, were in constant struggle over control of the land between South Carolina and Florida. American Indians, who were the original inhabitants of the area, also fought to retain or regain their occupied lands.

Africans, in the Americas against their will, were often caught in the middle of this international rivalry. Many Africans assessed the situation strategically, and enlisted the aid of Indians who were hostile to the English in the Carolinas. Many people escaped with Indian help from the English plantations to Spanish Florida, where freedom was possible.

The Spaniards themselves practiced slavery, and they were by no means free of racial discrimination. Eighteenth century Spanish law regarding slavery and manumission from slavery, however, was substantially different from English law, and was in many ways more flexible.

Slaves were permitted, for example, to earn money, buy their own freedom, and sue their masters in court. Owners were not allowed to break up families through sales. These laws, established in Spain during the thirteenth century, paved the way for the Spanish officials in Florida to develop their policy of sanctuary for escaped slaves.

In 1686, the Spaniards in St. Augustine began to spread the word that escaped slaves would be given religious sanctuary in Spanish Florida. Africans in the English colonies seized this opportunity immediately. The first recorded group of fugitives arrived in St. Augustine in 1687, and included eight men, two women, and a nursing child. By 1738, more than 100 African refugees had settled in St. Augustine, and in that year, they established a fort and community just north of the Spanish town.

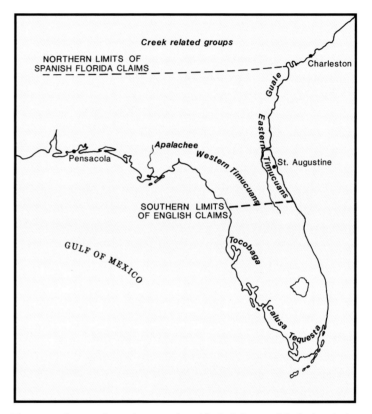

The territory between the two lines was claimed by both Spain and England in the late seventeenth and early eighteenth centuries. Also shown are the American Indian groups original to the area.

Warfare between England, France, and Spain raged throughout the Americas and in Europe during the eighteenth century, largely over the control of colonial territories and overseas trade.[1]

AFRICAN ORIGINS

The story of Mose began in Africa and Europe, hundreds of years before the founding of America. By 1700, some one and a half million African people had been brought unwillingly to the Americas as slaves.

When Europeans first arrived in West Africa, they found a diversity of people and cultures - nomadic tribes, rich trading societies, and powerful city-states. The mixture of these traditions in the Americas later produced a distinctively African-American cultural tradition, influenced by European and American Indian traditions, but profoundly rooted in the African past.

Costume from Loango.[3]

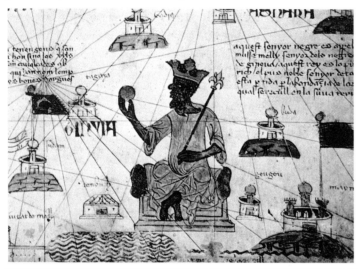

King of Mali.[2]

Life scenes from Cabo Verdo.[4]

The people at Mose came from a variety of West African areas, and they brought much of the rich and diverse cultures of the region with them to America - language, ideas, styles, traditions, religion and beliefs, technology, art and music.

The Court of the King of Iddah, Niger River.[5]

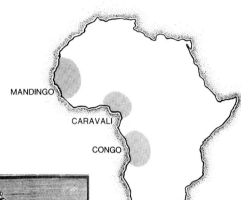

MANDINGO

CARAVALI

CONGO

The African King of Sestro meets with Europeans on the Windward Coast, in the area of modern Liberia.[6]

"Alkemy," King of Guinea.[7]

ALKEMY, ROY DE LA GVINEE

3

People from the Caravali (Calabar), Mandingo, Congo, and perhaps other West African culture areas were present at Mose. Other Africans in Spanish Florida came from still other African cultures, including people from not only Congo, Caravali, and Mandingo areas, but also Mina, Guinea, Gambia, and Arara areas (some of which were terms used by Europeans for the origin of slave shipments rather than actual cultural groups). They also came from Cuba, Jamaica, Barbados, Antigua, Venezuela, Colombia, and the Canary Islands.

This Congo initiation mask is used in a ceremony by boys reaching adulthood, and is also a charm that protects the initiate's future fertility.[8]

The Ijaw people live in small towns near Calabar in the Niger River delta, and are traders. This shrine object honors the water spirits that control the waterways enabling trade.[9]

This war tunic demonstrates the importance of the warrior and the role of Islam in Mandingo culture. It provided both practical and spiritual protection. The amulets are leather-covered scriptures from the Koran, and the charms are mystical "medicines" of local belief systems.[10]

The origins of African slavery in the Americas are found in Europe, and specifically in Moorish Iberia (today's Spain and Portugal).

Some Africans had been in Europe since the beginning of recorded history. The number of African people in Europe increased dramatically, however, after the Moorish invasion of Iberia. For 700 years - from the eighth until the fifteenth century - the Islamic Moors (the Spanish term for people from north Africa) occupied parts of Iberia. They were expelled from Portugal in 1250, but not from southern Spain until 1492. During that time, the Moors brought settlers and slaves of many nationalities, and the people of Spain became familiar with Africans, both slave and free, and with the practice of slavery.

Muslim soldiers, including Africans, invading Spain.[12]

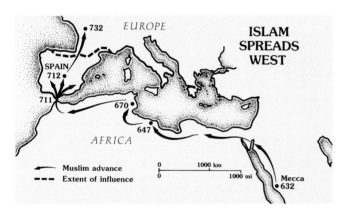

The route (with dates) of the Islamic Moors crossing North Africa and entering the Iberian peninsula.

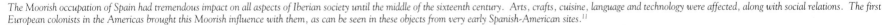

The Moorish occupation of Spain had tremendous impact on all aspects of Iberian society until the middle of the sixteenth century. Arts, crafts, cuisine, language and technology were affected, along with social relations. The first European colonists in the Americas brought this Moorish influence with them, as can be seen in these objects from very early Spanish-American sites.[11]

Consequence of a just war ... the laws of Spanish slavery

"Slaves" and "Africans" were not synonymous in Moorish Spain. Muslim people took slaves from wherever they conquered new lands. In Spain of 1492, there were slaves who were Jewish, Moorish, "Turkish" (actually Egyptians, Syrians and Lebanese); white Christians (Sardinians, Greeks, Russians); Canary Island natives (Guanches); and black Africans.

Moors (including blacks) enslaving white Christians and their livestock.[13]

Slavery was not defined by race in Moorish Spain. Here, black gentlemen playing chess are waited on by black and white servants.[14]

Laws governing slaves in Spain, and later in the Spanish colonies of America, were specifically based on the thirteenth century codes of the Castilian king, Alfonso X. Alfonso's laws, like Islamic laws and the earlier Justinian Code, were based on the assumption that slavery was an unnatural state, and that all people were born free. However, slavery was believed to justly occur as a consequence of war or refusal to accept the conquerors' religion. Slavery in Moorish Iberia was not a consequence of race or color.

The Spanish slave code provided certain rights for slaves. Slaves could buy their freedom, maintain family cohesiveness, and sue their masters for mistreatment. Governors and rulers often freed slaves as a reward for service to the Crown. After 1492, this slave code was brought to the Americas by the Spaniards, and underlaid many of the differences between the lives of some Spanish-African slaves and the lives of many slaves in the English colonies. It also led to the establishment of Fort Mose.

The "Siete Partidas", a compendium of Spanish law, laid down the policies regarding slavery. These two pages include a discussion on the principles of freedom (left), and one on slavery (right).[16]

Africans in Europe were gradually integrated into Christianity, even to the extent that it was possible to reach sainthood. St. Maurice was a black saint popular in parts of Europe during the sixteenth century, and was the patron saint of the Holy Roman Empire.

King Alfonso X and his court.[15]

Thirteenth century Spanish Christians baptizing a black man.[17]

St. Maurice[18]

SLAVERY IN IBERIA AFTER THE MOORS

The African slave trade became important in Europe during the fifteenth century.

After the expulsion of the Moors from Portugal in 1250, the Portuguese lost a main source of labor - Moorish prisoners of war. The Portuguese ruler, Prince Henry the Navigator, opened the African trade in about 1440, and found slaves to be one of the most lucrative commodities for trade with Europe, along with gold, ivory and spices. The Portuguese soon controlled the slave trade in Iberia, and later, in the Americas during the early decades of European settlement.

Catholic popes ruled in Papal bulls of 1454 (Nicholas V) and 1456 (Calixtus III) that enslavement of Africans was justified on the grounds that it would bring them Christianity. The idea of enslaving people to bring them Christianity was carried to the Americas by the first Spanish conquistadors. Although Queen Isabella of Spain declared that Indian slavery was unlawful, the enslavement of American Indians was justified on the grounds that they refused to accept Christianity, or that they purportedly practiced cannibalism, which was believed contrary to the wishes of God.

Portuguese slave hunters using weapons and dogs to capture Africans.[20]

An African king receiving Portuguese men.[19]

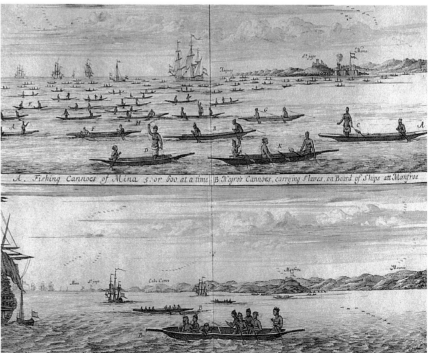

Africans in canoes carrying other Africans as slaves to European ships.[21]

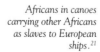

The first slaves in the Americas were not African, and the first Africans in the Americas were not slaves.

Black sailors, soldiers, servants and settlers arrived in the Americas in the fifteenth century, along with the earliest Europeans. These first black colonists were from Spain rather than Africa, and were known as ladinos.

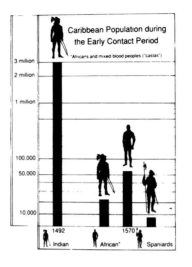

> Juan las Canarias was a black sailor who served on Columbus' flagship, the Santa Maria, during the first transatlantic voyage in 1492.

Juan las Canarias[22]

The first slaves to make the long journey across the Atlantic were Caribbean Indians enslaved by Columbus, and sent to Ferdinand and Isabella's court in 1495.

The King of Spain looks on as Columbus encounters a group of American Indians.[23]

Caribbean Indian population declined rapidly after first contact with Europeans.

"Spanish Cruelties Cause the Indians to Despair."[24]

An American Tragedy

The Indian population of Spanish America could not withstand the introduction of such common European diseases as measles, smallpox, influenza and the cold, since they had never been exposed to them before, and thus had no resistance. The Indians died by the thousands from these diseases, as well as from the terrible disruption to their society caused by warfare and enslavement. By the early 1520's the Indian population of much of the Caribbean was nearly extinct, and the Spaniards were desperate for a source of labor in the mines, fields, ranches and cities.

As a consequence of the disappearance of the Indians, millions of Africans came to be enslaved and brought unwillingly to the Americas.

Africans enslaved in the mines.[25]

Evidence from the Earth

As Indian populations declined, Spaniards began to exploit Africans for slave labor. This trend can be seen at the Spanish site of Puerto Real in Haiti (1503-1578), excavated by University of Florida archaeologists. The Spanish settlers initially used traditional Taino ceramic cookware. After about 1525, Taino cookware was replaced by a new type which was less like Taino and European pottery and more similar to hemispherical bowls produced by African potters. Archaeologists believe that this change in cooking pottery reflects the replacement of an Indian labor force by an African labor force.

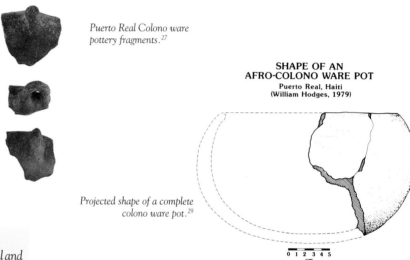

Puerto Real Colono ware pottery fragments.[27]

SHAPE OF AN AFRO-COLONO WARE POT
Puerto Real, Haiti
(William Hodges, 1979)

Projected shape of a complete colono ware pot.[29]

0 1 2 3 4 5
cm

A Rich Taino Legacy

At the time of Columbus' arrival, the Taino Indians of the Caribbean had sophisticated cultural and artistic traditions, reflected in their material world. By 1520, the drastic decline in Taino population, and the accompanying social collapse that occurred as a result of contact with Europeans, caused their arts to largely disappear, although their influence persists in traditional Spanish Caribbean craft traditions.

Clay "adorno" figures from ceramic pots, polished stone celts, clay stamp for decorating cotton, stone beads, stone zemi figure.[26]

Puerto Real map.[28]

SLAVES OF DISEASE: VICTIMS OF HEALTH

Africans were the only group in the Americas of 1500 with resistance to the diseases of three continents.

Centuries of intermittent contact between Europe and Africa had exposed the people of the African continent to European diseases, and because of this, the African newcomers to America were able to resist many of the common European diseases that were lethal to the Indians.

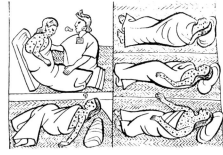

Smallpox struck the Indians of Mexico during the invasion of Cortés.[30]

Africans had another health advantage in coastal lowland areas, where much of the demand for labor was concentrated. This was the sickle cell trait. The sickle cell trait is a blood component that provides some protection against malaria. Although the sickle cell trait is also responsible for a relatively high incidence of the deadly sickle cell anemia among people of African heritage, the protection provided against malaria outweighed this disadvantage in the population's health. It also made the earliest African immigrants to the Caribbean the only people with resistance to malaria, which struck down both Europeans and Indians in large numbers after it was introduced to the Americas through early European contact.

The physical inability of both Europeans and American Indians to either adapt to or withstand the new disease climate of sixteenth century America was tragically fateful for African Americans. By the 1550's in the Americas, black skin came to be mentally associated with hard physical labor. Social attitudes and controls quickly developed to institutionalize this idea, and this is perhaps the most devastating legacy of the encounter for black Americans today.

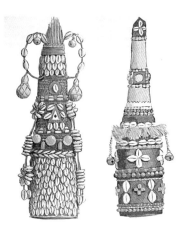

These ornate objects are used by African Brazilians during rituals to appease Omolu, the god of pestilence. Among the Yoruba in West Africa, this deity (known as Obaluaiye) has been both revered and feared for centuries as the god able to heal or to conjure smallpox.[31]

Slaves working in an early sugar mill in the Antilles. Sugar was a major agricultural enterprise in the Americas, and required large numbers of workers.[33]

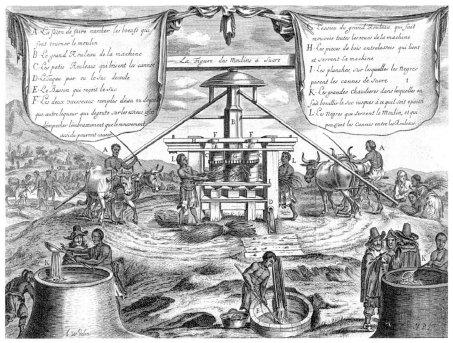

In Africa, Osanyin is the Yoruba god of herbal medicine, helping to cure worshippers of diseases like smallpox. He is a small figure with one eye, one arm, and one leg. In Cuba his name became Osain. This statue and ritual staff were made in Miami by Afro-Cubans.[32]

BLACK EXPLORERS AND CONQUISTADORS

People of African heritage accompanied all of the first Spanish expeditions, often playing important military and diplomatic roles.

The ambivalent and often confusing position of Africans - both free and unfree - in the early Spanish colonies is well-illustrated by these black explorers and soldiers. They marched, fought, and scouted. Some, even while slaves themselves, were rewarded for their valor with landed estates and large number of Indian slaves. For many Native Americans, these African explorers were among the first Old World people they met - simply conquistadors of another color.

Juan Valiente: Conqueror and Slave [35]

Juan Valiente was a black slave who came to the Americas with his master, Alonso Valiente. With Alonso's permission, he joined various expeditions and fought fiercely with Spanish soldiers in Guatemala, Peru, and Chile. In 1546 the governor of Chile gave him a large estate in recognition of his valor, and a few years later he was given several Indian towns which had to pay him tribute. He married a free black woman, Juana de Valdivia, and was killed in action in 1553, still a slave. After his death, his master sued to claim all of the property and tribute that had been acquired by Valiente.

Juan Garrido: Free Black Explorer

Juan Garrido was a free African who made his way from Seville, Spain, to Hispaniola around 1496. He became well known for his exploits with Ponce de León's Caribbean expeditions, and later joined Cortés in Mexico, fighting in the epic battles at Tenochtitlán. This sixteenth century engraving shows Garrido with Cortés meeting two Mexican officials. [34]

Esteban: Explorer and Survivor

Esteban was a gunbearer, scout, slave and soldier with Pánfilo de Narváez in his 1528 expedition to Florida. Esteban was one of only four survivors out of the original group of 400. He spent eight years walking overland from Florida to Mexico City, and was probably the first non-Indian person seen by many Native Americans. After arriving in Mexico, he served as a guide to missionaries in the southwestern U.S. region, and was killed in a Zuni town on the upper Rio Grande in 1538.

Coronado expedition

A free black Spaniard served as the interpreter on Coronado's expedition through southwestern North America in 1540. He, along with two other Africans, stayed behind in New Mexico when Coronado returned to Mexico. The interpreter lived with missionaries at Quivira, and eventually became a Franciscan friar.

African resistance to slavery in the Americas was immediate, widespread and often successful.

Almost immediately upon arriving in the Americas, African slaves rebelled against their forced servitude. Slave uprisings and rebellions took place in Santo Domingo in 1522, in Mexico in 1523; in the South Carolina colony of Vásquez de Allyón in 1526, in Cuba in 1530, and the five year old capital of Colombia was destroyed by slave rebellions in 1530. Slave rebellions occurred regularly throughout Spanish America until the ninteenth century.

Maroons in Surinam waged a serious, multi-year war against the European colonists in the late eighteenth century. Englishman John Stedman recounted his experiences in the war, and William Blake provided the illustrations. (Top: "A Rebel Negro Armed and on his guard;" Center: "Death of a rebel slave;" Bottom: "A Coromantyn Free Negro, or Ranger, armed.")[37]

Despite the sadistic punishments imposed on runaways, large numbers of slaves escaped to inhospitable parts of the swamps and mountains. There they formed runaway communities, known variously as "cimarron," "palenque," or "maroon" towns. Africans in these towns were often allied with the Indians of the region, and these Afro-Indian communities waged successful guerilla warfare against the European towns and settlers. In several areas their efforts so plagued the Spaniards that from the sixteenth century onward, peace treaties were made, and amnesty and freedom were granted to the cimarrones.

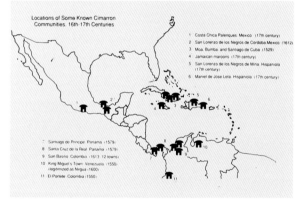

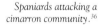
Spaniards attacking a cimarron community.[36]

This portrait of Jamaican maroon captain Leonard Parkinson was drawn from life in 1796 by artist Raimback. Many captured Jamaican maroons were exiled to Nova Scotia.[38]

An African polity in the New World

From the early decades of the sixteenth century, enslaved African mine workers in Colombia escaped to what is today Ecuador. Many took refuge with the Manbi and Mantux Indian tribes of the northern Ecuador coast. The descendants of these Africans and Indians became the tribal chiefs, establishing a headquarters known as "El Portete," from which they waged unceasing war on the Spaniards. They were recognized as free and legitimate by the Spaniards in 1598.

Detail from painting Zambo Chiefs in Ecuador.[39]

HISPANIOLA

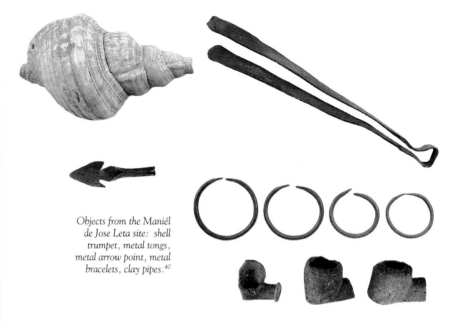

Objects from the Maniél de Jose Leta site: shell trumpet, metal tongs, metal arrow point, metal bracelets, clay pipes.[40]

Maniél de Jose Leta - A rebel town in Hispaniola

Archaeologists Manuel García Arévalo and Jose Arrom in the Dominican Republic have located evidence for at least one early cimarron town, called Maniél de Jose Leta. It was occupied during the seventeenth century by a group of Africans and African-Indians. Some 600 families of fugitive slaves - more than 2,000 people - lived in four cimarron towns in the region. They were described in 1662 by Bishop Francisco de la Cueba Maldonado, who lamented that although some were Catholics and had crosses in their houses, they had no priest and "committed idolatries."

The people hunted feral pigs, made iron tools and implements, farmed, and panned for gold which they used to buy wine, supplies and clothes from blacks in Santo Domingo. They used Indian pottery and Spanish pottery, as well as other pottery that appears to have African influence and may have been made in the cimarron town. Clay pipes with African designs were found at the site. They also worked in iron and copper, making bracelets, arrowheads, nails and other implements. In 1666 the community was attacked and destroyed by the Spanish military authorities, and was lost until its rediscovery by archaeologists in 1980.

A NEW SOCIAL ORDER

Although the majority of Africans in the colonies were forced into slavery, there was always a consistent segment of Spanish colonial society made up of free black people.

Many free people of African heritage in the Spanish colonies were craftspeople, laborers, soldiers, artisans and merchants. Although the majority of these people married others of African descent, many of them married whites, Indians, and mixed-blood mates. A multi-racial and multi-ethnic society quickly emerged throughout Latin America, the Caribbean, and Florida. It was the first truly new, hybrid ethnic group of the post-Columbus world, and is today still the major social group in Latin America.

A Spanish colonial administrator invites a mestizo, a mulatto, and an Indian for supper. This drawing, done by a Peruvian mestizo (person of mixed Indian-European heritage), characterizes the mixed racial nature of Spanish Peruvian colonial society.[41]

People of mixed African-European-Indian ancestry were known as "Castas" in Spanish colonial society. The Spaniards developed a highly organized, detailed system for identifying the precise genetic heritage of an individual, as this painting from eighteenth century Mexico illustrates.[42]

AFRICAN PEOPLE IN THE COLONIAL SOUTHEAST

The first African settlers in what is now the United States came to South Carolina in 1526.

The Spanish explorer Vásquez de Allyón established the town of San Miguel de Gualdape near present-day Sapelo Sound in Georgia. Some 500 Spaniards and 100 African laborers came with him. The colony failed after two months because of illness, Indian hostility and a slave rebellion. Although the Spanish colonists abandoned the colony, many of the Africans escaped to the forests and chose to remain there in freedom with the Indians.

People of African heritage were always part of the colonial experience in the southeastern U.S.

The Southeast was a relatively remote, international frontier during the seventeenth and eighteenth centuries. Because of its isolation, instability and relative scarcity of human resources, there was more opportunity and flexibility on the frontier for everyone - black, red or white.

In Spanish Florida, African people had been part of the colony of St. Augustine since its establishment in 1565. They came from the Caribbean and South America as well as from Africa. Most African Floridians lived in St. Augustine, scattered throughout the town. They were both free and unfree, and probably made up about ten percent of the town's population.

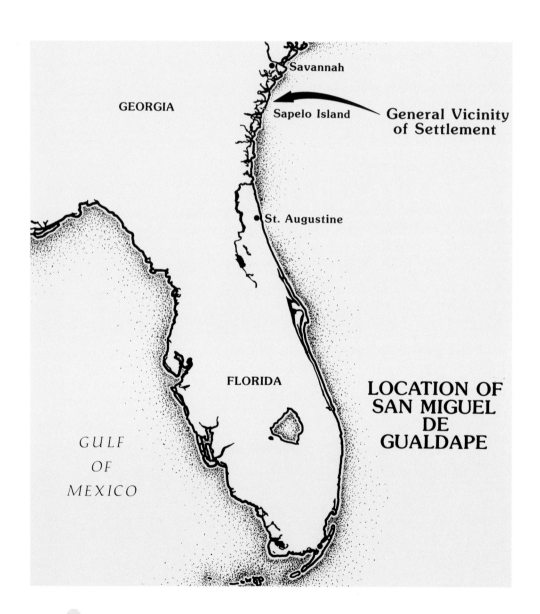

One hundred and fifty years after the Allyón colony, many more Africans came in bondage to the southern English colonies, most often to work on the cotton, indigo, rice and tobacco plantations established after 1670 in the Carolinas.

During the period from about 1690 to 1720, there were probably more than 15,000 black residents in South Carolina - the majority of all non-Native people.

An Evil Traffic

In the early years of South Carolina's settlement, many black and white residents came from the Caribbean. By the beginning of the eighteenth century, however, the majority of the unfree black people in South Carolina came directly from Africa, as victims of the slave trade. The journey itself was hellish, and thousands of those packed into the ships perished before reaching America.

These objects were excavated from the slave ship Henrietta Marie, which sunk off the Marquesas Islands around 1700. The ship carried trade goods from both Europe and Africa, along with hundreds of slave shackles. Bars of "voyage iron" were used as trading currency in Africa and the Americas, and may have been used to make and repair slave shackles on board, as suggested by the iron post anvil. We know that in 1703 the price of slaves in Calabar (the homeland of several Mose residents) was 12 bars for a man and 9 bars for a woman.

Sailors throwing slaves overboard.[44]

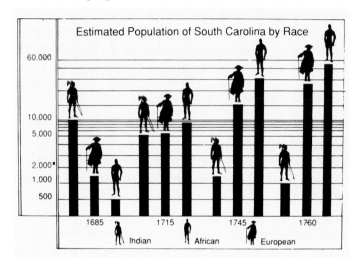

Estimated Population of South Carolina by Race

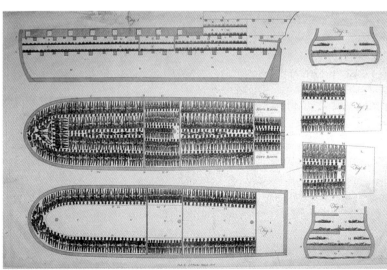

Diagram of a slave ship.[43]

Slave wrist shackles, iron post anvil, African ivory tusk, European glass trade beads, "voyage iron" bar.[45]

An Unacknowledged Legacy

Life and economy in the early Carolinas depended almost entirely upon black labor and skill, and unfree African workers sustained life on the plantation. They not only performed the necessary labor, but also brought with them from Africa many of the traditions and technologies for farming, fishing, building construction, and a variety of other trades and crafts. Many of these have persisted until today as important - but often unrecognized - African contributions to American life.

Rice became an important crop along the coastal lowlands of English Carolina at the end of the seventeenth century. African slaves who had been rice farmers in their homeland introduced the technology of rice cultivation. This encouraged the importation of skilled African rice farmers as slaves.[46]

African (left)[47] and African-American (right)[48] grain mortars, often used for rice, were very similar, as were the baskets used to "fan" rice.

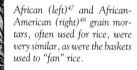

Rebellion and Escape

Africans in bondage in South Carolina - like those in the earlier Spanish colonies - rebelled immediately against enslavement. As the largest segment of colonial population in the Carolinas, they posed an alarming potential threat to the white minority. Rebellions took place in 1711, 1714, and 1739, and slaves attempted escape at tremendous risk almost constantly. A runaway slave community was established in the area of Dismal Swamp, North Carolina, and has never been found to this day.

Most Africans in South Carolina lived on large rural plantations, isolated from Euro-American population centers. Most of their social interaction was with other African people, and much was with American Indians. A communication network developed among black workers in the Southeast, through which people on the plantations of Carolina learned that freedom was granted to those who reached the Spanish colony of Florida and converted to Catholicism.

A Cimarron haven in Florida

Fort Mose, although legally sanctioned by the Spaniards in Florida, would have seemed like a Cimarron ("runaway") community to the English in South Carolina. Mose did prove, in fact, to be a symbol of hope for many Africans in the English Colony.

Most plantations were located on rivers or the coast, and transportation by boat was common. Many African slaves were skilled watermen, carrying their boating and fishing practices from Africa to the Americas. Plantation owners valued these skills, and often employed the skilled Africans at building dugout canoes, piloting boats, transporting goods, and fishing for the plantation. Access to boats also gave Africans the opportunity to interact with Indians and others outside the plantation, to learn news, and to assist runaways and escape themselves.[49]

"GIVING LIBERTY TO ALL"

The policy of giving religious sanctuary to escaped slaves was Spanish Florida's creative solution to a number of local problems.

Welcoming the refugees served to strike an economic blow at the English colonies, while at the same time adding skilled workers and Catholic converts to the Spanish colonies. Formal legal sanction for this policy came in 1693, when King Charles II of Spain issued a royal proclamation on the status of runaways to Florida, "...giving liberty to all...the men as well as the women...so that by their example and by my liberality others will do the same..."

Word of the Spanish policy spread rapidly among the black population in the Carolinas, and the number of escapees to Florida steadily increased. Battling slavecatchers, hunger and dangerous swamps, they created the first American underground railroad, more than a century before the Civil War.

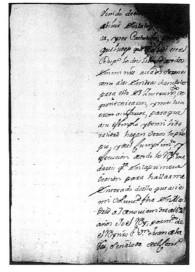

Reproduction of 1693 royal proclamation.[50]

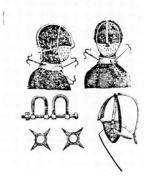

A front and profile view of an African's head, with the mouth-piece and necklace, the hooks round which are placed to prevent an escape when pursued in the woods, and to hinder them from laying down the head to procure rest.—At A is a flat iron which goes into the mouth, and so effectually keeps down the tongue, that nothing can be swallowed, not even the saliva, a passage for which is made through holes in the mouth-plate.

An enlarged view of the mouth-piece, which, when long worn, becomes so heated, as frequently to bring off the skin along with it.

A view of the leg-bolts or shackles, as put upon the legs of the slaves on ship-board, in the middle passage.

An enlarged view of the boots and spurs, as used at some plantations in Antigua.

Devices such as those depicted here were often used to control slaves in the Americas, especially slaves who had attempted escape.[51]

Angry Words

The Spanish fugitive slave policy, and the events it provoked, greatly aggravated the English colonists in Carolina. Their letters and speeches - written at the time - reflect this aggravation:

Letter from Englishman William Dunlop to the Governor of Florida, 1688...

Those people who came from this province [St. Augustine] and hostilly invaded the province of Carolina In the months of Agust and December In An: 1686 did kill and destroy two men; and did cary away prisoners 5 more persons of his Majesty's Subjects: 11 Negroe slaves: did burn and destroy th. town of Stuartstown in Port Royall; Kill the cattell and Hogs of his Majesty's subjects there: cary away and destroy their gold plate and other goods to the value of sixteen thousand peeces of Eight beside the damage done others of his Majesty's Subjects by being alarmed and disturbed to a far greater Value.

South Carolina House of Assembly Records, July 23, 1740...

It is with great Reason, we apprehend, that that Part of our Calamities, proceeding from the frequent Attempts of our Slaves, arises from the Designs and Intrigues of our Enemies the Spaniards in St. Augustine and Florida, who have had the Ruin and Destruction of these your Majesty's Colonies of South Carolina and Georgia long in View. Witness ... a Proclamation published at St. Augustine, in his Catholic Majesty's Name, promising Freedom and other Encouragement to all slaves that should desert from your Majesty's Subjects of this Province and join them. In Consequence of which Proclamation, many have already deserted, and others encouraged daily to do the same; and even those who have committed the most inhuman Murders, are there harboured, entertained and caressed.

South Carolina Report of the Committee of Conference on the Case of the Negroes' Desertion to St. Augustine, April 2, 1739....

That an Encouragement be given to white Men and free Indian for taking up and bringing in all Negro Slaves that are already deserted or shall hereafter desert from this province according to the rates and proportions following, to wit,

For Negro men taken up beyond the Savannah River and brought home alive the sum of 40 Lb a piece,

For women taken and brought as above 25 Lb each,

For children under the age of 12 years 10 Lb each, which sums shall be paid by their respective owners.

And that an encouragement be given for bringing in the scalps of such men and women Negro slaves that are already deserted or shall hereafter desert who shall be found beyond the Savannah River and cannot be taken and brought home alive, to wit, for each scalp with the two ears 20 Lb. to be paid out of the Publick Treasury. Such Negroes as shall be executed for the desertion of their owners shall be reimbursed by the Publick.

THE ESTABLISHMENT OF MOSE: A FORTRESS OF FREEDOM

By 1738, more than 100 African fugitives had reached St. Augustine. In that year, the Spanish government established the fort and community of Gracia Real de Santa Teresa de Mose about 2 miles north of the town.

Upon their arrival in St. Augustine, many of the male fugitives from Carolina were made members of the Spanish slave militia, and in 1738 they formed a free black company. The Captain of the Mose militia was Francisco Menendez, who had first been appointed Captain of the St. Augustine slave militia in 1726. Like the other Mose officers, Menendez was an escaped slave.

The recently freed soldiers moved to the frontier with their families, where they built Fort Mose and a small adjacent town. The fort was built about two miles north of St. Augustine, across marsh and open land. In 1738, there were 38 households of men, women and children at Mose.

Fort Mose served as a beacon of liberty for enslaved Carolinians, and protected the Spanish colony against English attack.

Rumors of their situation spread back to South Carolina and circulated among the many Africans still enslaved on coastal plantations. In September 1739, black workers at Stono near Charleston launched the largest slave uprising in the history of the North American colonies. Scores of armed slaves joined forces and began marching toward Florida and possible freedom, before white militia crushed the revolt.

Fort Mose quickly came to represent freedom to countless African Americans in South Carolina, where roughly 40,000 enslaved blacks outnumbered 20,000 white colonists by two to one. After the Stono Rebellion of 1739, authorities in Charleston blamed the Spanish, then at war with England, for helping to incite the uprising.

The soldiers at Fort Mose had more than symbolic value for Florida. With only several thousand Europeans and several hundred Africans, the small Spanish colony needed strong defenses, and the black militia at Fort Mose represented an important force. Having escaped from Carolina, these African Americans knew the region well, and would fight to the death if their former English masters invaded from the north.

Mose was one of a number of frontier outposts constructed during the eighteenth century to defend St. Augustine.

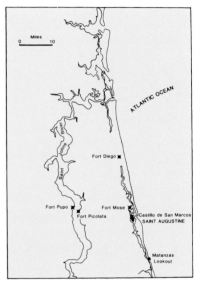

This map shows the fortifications which protected St. Augustine in the early eighteenth century. Fort Mose was the northernmost offical fortress protecting Spanish Florida. Farther north, Ft. Diego was actually the fortified home of the mulatto cattle rancher Diego de Espinosa and was often used as a remote outpost.

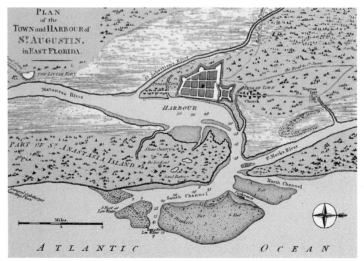

The Thomas Jefferys map of 1762, showing what Fort Mose (labelled "Negroe Fort") looked like in 1740.[52]

The original fort was a small, twenty-meter-square enclosure, containing a watchtower, a well and a guardhouse. Its walls were of earth, stakes and cactus, and it was surrounded by a shallow moat. It was probably similar to other eighteenth century Spanish Florida forts of the same size.

When it was first occupied by the black company, the fort was on dry land adjacent to a creek. Today the site of the original fort is under water, the result of sea level rise and development in the wetlands environment.

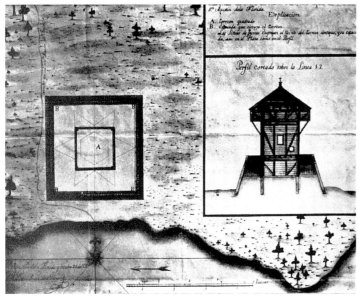

These two forts, Pupo[53] and Picolata[54], were constructed during the same period as Fort Mose, and served as outposts on the St. Johns River to the west of St. Augustine. The original Fort Mose resembled Pupo and Picolata in layout, and was probably similar in other details as well.

This aerial photograph taken in 1987 shows the area of the first Fort Mose, which is today a wetland of tidal creeks and marshes. The fort itself is now under water, in approximately the area encircled on the map.

View of the First Fort

A description of the original fort was made during Oglethorpe's raid on Mose in 1740 (A Report to the South Carolina General Assembly):

Fort Moosa ... being about twenty Miles from Fort Diego within two Miles' Distance and in full Sight of St. Augustine (lying near the Creek which runs up between that and Point Cartell up to Fort Diego) was made in the Middle of a Plantation for Safety of the Negroes against Indians. It was four Square with a Flanker at each Corner, banked round with Earth, having a Ditch without on all Sides lined round with prickly Palmeto Royal and had a Well and House within, and a Look Out.

Destruction of the first Fort Mose

In 1740, two years after the start of the Mose community and one year after the Stono Uprising in Carolina, English forces attacked St. Augustine, led by General James Oglethorpe of Georgia.

War between Spain and England raised the possibility that the Spanish in Florida might mount an attack on Georgia or encourage another rebellion among the black majority in Carolina. The English thus sought to strike first. Oglethorpe led a large but clumsy attack against St. Augustine, using colonial soldiers from Georgia and Carolina, as well as Indian allies.

During the attack, Fort Mose was captured. All of the Mose inhabitants reached the safety of the Castillo de San Marcos in St. Augustine, where they took refuge along with the rest of St. Augustine's population. Oglethorpe's men occupied Fort Mose during their siege of St. Augustine, but were defeated there in a pitched battle with the black, white and Indian Spanish forces. Fort Mose was badly damaged in the battle, and the community was abandoned for twelve years.

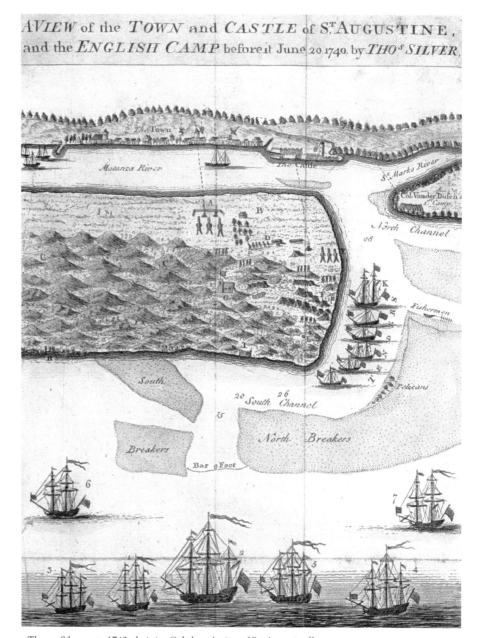

Thomas Silver map, 1740, depicting Oglethorpe's siege of St. Augustine.[55]

URBAN INTERLUDE, 1740-1752

During the twelve year period between the destruction of the first fort and the construction of the second fort, the inhabitants of Fort Mose lived in St. Augustine among the Spanish, Indian, and other African residents of the town.

While they were in St. Augustine, the people from Mose worked in a variety of occupations. Several of the Mose soldiers - including Captain Francisco Menendez - signed on as "privateers" for the Spanish. Their skill as watermen was useful in capturing British ships to help obtain much-needed goods for the colony.

Some black women in St. Augustine sold foods, such as baked goods and honey, from their homes. Other members of the black community provided skilled labor for the town as blacksmiths, charcoal burners, carpenters and musicians. Some also worked in the cattle industry and as frontier scouts and interpreters.

This design appeared on the reverse of the handmade St. Christopher's medal found at Mose. It depicts the compass directions in a traditional seafaring style, and may have been used by an African waterman.[56]

Isavel de los Rios was a free black woman who lived in St. Augustine and sold fresh baked "rosquetes" (spiral rolls), sugar syrup, and possibly other provisions from her home. We know of Isavel and of Captain Chrispin de Tapia, a free black man who ran a grocery store, through court records. Both provisioners testified in a 1695 court case against several Apalachee Indians that the Indians had given them counterfeit money for the purchase of rolls and other goods. We also know that in 1683, de Tapia was listed as a corporal in the St. Augustine black militia. (Stetson Collection, P.K. Yonge Library of Florida History, leg. 157A, folios 193-205; AGI SD 226)

African Blacksmith

Juan Merino was a 46 year old free African blacksmith who came to St. Augustine from Havana as a convict in 1675. He worked as a master charcoal burner in the royal forge, burning charcoal and making and repairing weapons. By 1683 he had opened his own forge where he did blacksmithing for the royal armorer and private citizens. Merino was also listed as second lieutenant in the St. Augustine black militia in 1683.

Quote from ex-Governor de Hita Salazar in 1683:

"...If we had not gotten a black convict from Havana and a mulatto exiled from Havana, both of whom know something of weapons and charcoal making, we would have found ourselves in necessity." (Connor document collections Reel 3; AGI SD 54-5-14-159, 6-28-1683; P.K. Yonge Library of Florida History; AGI SD 226)

Blacksmithing was a common occupation for African Americans. In Africa, the smith was an honored and powerful figure in the community. These images show a nineteenth century Congo blacksmith, and the bellows used to stoke the fire.[57]

FORT MOSE RESURRECTED

In 1752 the town and fort at Mose were rebuilt at a slightly different location. The former residents, who were by then well-settled into town life, moved reluctantly back to the frontier under pressure from the Spanish authorities who still needed Mose as the colony's first line of defense against the English.

The new fort was a walled enclosure with a moat, containing a number of buildings. It was much larger than the first fort, about 65 meters to a side, and was open on one side along the creek. The walls of Mose were made of packed earth, faced with clay and sod, and were planted with cactus. The moat was 6 feet wide and two feet deep, and was probably also planted with cactus.

The fort was surrounded by fields, farmed by the people of Mose. They lived in palm-thatch houses, which initially at least were built inside the protective walls of the fort.

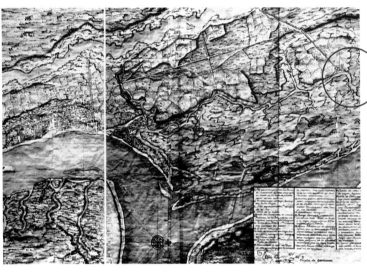

This map of St. Augustine shows Fort Mose as it looked in 1763. Note the buildings which were inside the fort walls, the defense line which extends from the fort, and the nearby planted fields.[58]

Reconstruction of the second Fort Mose.[59]

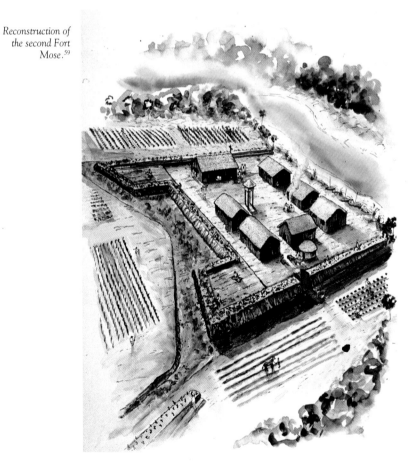

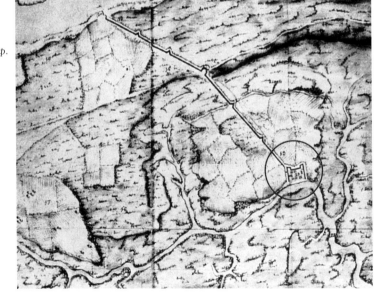

Detail of 1763 map.

Solana report

An eye-witness account of Ft. Mose was recorded in 1759, made by the Franciscan priest Father Juan Joseph de Solana, who was reporting on the conditions in St. Augustine in that year:

The Fort at Mose is situated on the banks of the River which runs to the north, and at a distance of 3/4 of a league from the presidio, the part that faces the river has no protection of defense whatsoever and is formed by two small bastions which look landward on which are mounted two four-pound cannons and six swivel guns divided among them … the earthwork embankment is covered with thorns and the moat is three feet wide and two feet deep … the housing which it includes are some huts of thatch, the chapel is ten varas long and six wide, the walls which are under construction are made of wood and the sacristy, which is finished, and in which the priest lives, is a very small room and serves as the chapel for the fort.

Artillery at Fort Mose

An inventory from the colonial archives of Spain lists the types of artillery present at Fort Mose in 1759. These included:

Iron Cannons, 3 pounders, mounted on carriages - fair condition	2
Iron swivel guns of half a pound - good condition	4
Equipment sets for the cannons - fair condition	2
Equipment sets for the swivel guns - fair condition	4
Cannon balls for the cannons	14
Shot for the swivel guns	28
Pounds of Gunpowder - good condition	40
Pounds of Matchcord for firing ordinance - fair condition	12
Cloth cartridges for charges of gunpowder - fair condition	14
Cloth cartridges for grapeshot - fair condition	14
Cloth cartridges for powder for the swivel guns	28
Cloth cartridges for grapeshot for the muskets	28
Gunpowder horn with firing pins - good condition	2
Large chests or bins for storing munitions	2
Muskets - fair condition	24

Report by the Captain of Artillery, Don Manuel de Barros, April 20, 1759 (Archivo General de Indias, Seville; SD 2604).

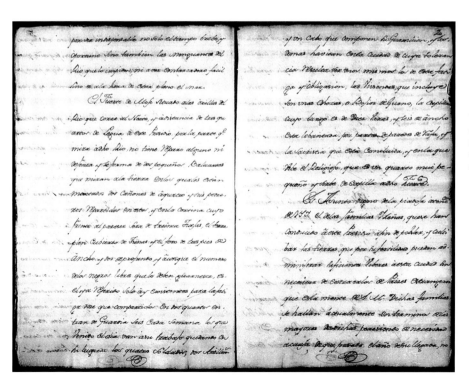

This is the most detailed known description of the town of Fort Mose, written by Father Solana in 1759.[60]

Photograph of the original Mose artillery inventory.[61]

Spanish Guns of the Eighteenth Century
Weapons were essential to survival on the Spanish frontier. The soldiers of Mose used military issue weapons in their defense of the fort. Gunflints and musket balls were the only military items excavated from the fort site. The weapons shown here are from other eighteenth century sites in Spanish Florida.

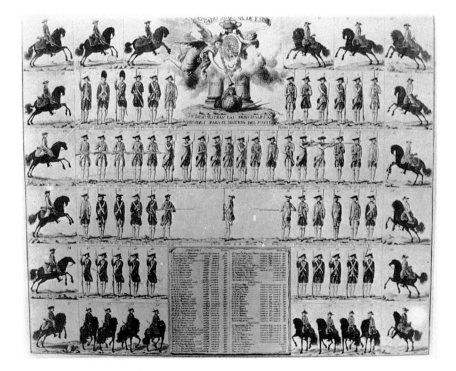

The flintlock rifles used at Mose would have resembled those used at other Spanish Florida sites. (Flintlock Musket barrel, lock, butt stock, butt plate; Socket Bayonet for Musket; Wooden Ramrod and Brass Holder; Ramrod Tip)[63]

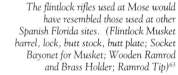

Eighteenth century image of the principle postures used in handling the flintlock rifle.[62]

Flintlock pistols would also have been used at Mose. Shown here from a shipwreck is a cast poured in the limerock which formed around the pistol, the original gun having dissolved, and a preserved wooden pistol stock.[64]

Soldiers usually made their own musket balls by pouring molten lead into molds, as shown in this seventeenth century image.[66]

Flintlock guns required a variety of accessories. Powder was kept in sacks of leather with metal nozzles and valves that measured out the correct amount. Depending on the size of the gun, different sizes of lead balls were fired, and gunflints made by soldiers provided the spark to ignite the powder and shoot the gun (balls and flints from Fort Mose).[65]

BLACK MILITIA IN THE SPANISH COLONIES

Soldiers of African heritage were regularly enlisted in colonial militias throughout the Spanish colonies.

Black Spaniards, including people originally from Africa and those born in Spain and the Americas, were a significant force in the defense of the Spanish colonies. Black militias were important as early as the sixteenth century.

Many of the black militias were "disciplined militia," and members were trained, had special uniforms, and received salaries. Militia members were free, and the officers were black, although a white officer conducted periodic reviews. These militias were active throughout the Spanish colonies, including Cuba, Puerto Rico, Hispaniola, Florida, Mexico, Panamá, Venezuela, Colombia, Peru, and Guatemala.

Late eighteenth century image of a Panamanian artilleryman.[69]

African militia members appear in this eighteenth century scene of a procession in Mexico City's main square.[70]

These two free black militia members include an officer from Veracruz (left) and a soldier from Havana (right), ca. 1770-1776.[67]

Seventeenth century image of a Puerto Rican soldier.[68]

Mulatto infantry from the Yucatán, 1767.[71]

Soldier in a black company of a volunteer infantry, Santo Domingo, 1785.[72]

Two soldiers from free black disciplined militia in Cuba, 1795.[73]

Brazilian infantry drummer, 1773.[74]

Black militias were also present in Spain's Asian colonies. This late eighteenth century image shows garrisons of Manila and Cavite, in the Philippines, including one black soldier representing a unit of 100 men.[75]

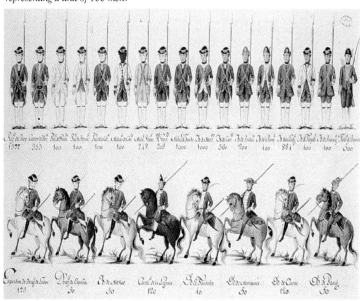

Some militias were based in Spain but did service in the Americas, as did these eighteenth century soldiers.[76]

Spain was not the only colonial power to enlist Africans for military service. These soldiers were stationed in eighteenth century French St. Domingue (on the island of Hispaniola), and black soldiers were present in many other colonial militias as well.[77]

The Fort Mose militia was a community-based free black militia. The St. Augustine garrison also had a black company as early as 1683. Its members came from throughout Latin America and Africa, and included both free blacks and slaves. Some officers, in fact, were slaves. Black soldiers in colonial Florida served in military maneuvers and often performed the critical functions of scouting and information gathering on the frontier, sometimes alone and sometimes in groups including Indians and Spanish soldiers.

Although uniforms were not supplied to the soldiers at Mose, at least some individuals, like Captain Francisco Menendez, must have acquired and worn the uniform of the St. Augustine militia.

Francisco Menendez, the Captain of the Mose militia, was a determined individual. Historical documents have revealed much about this remarkable man, a West African Mandingo by birth and former English slave who escaped to St. Augustine with the aid of the Yamassee Indians. His varied actions included writing letters to the King of Spain demanding fair payment, and serving as a corsair on a Spanish privateer ship, only to be captured by the English and reenslaved in Nassau. Documents show that somehow Menendez made his way back to St. Augustine to once again oversee the Mose militia. In 1763, Menendez, with his Mandingo wife and their four children, moved to Cuba with the rest of the Florida colonists and settled in the Matanzas province.

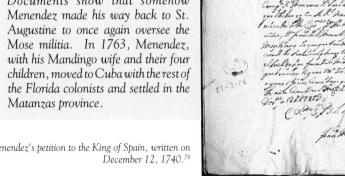

Menendez's petition to the King of Spain, written on December 12, 1740.[78]

LIFE AT MOSE: A CULTURAL CROSSROAD

The Mose community was a colorful mosaic of people of varied origins and experiences.

Many of the Mose residents, like Captain Francisco Menendez, were originally from Africa. They came from various West African cultures, and after coming to America, these same people lived with the English, the Indians, and the Spaniards. Their African-American compatriots in Florida were from all over Latin America. The town would have been filled with the sounds and sights of many languages and cultures.

An African-American community in the West Indies.[79]

The blending of cultures in Brazil - European dress, African techniques of carrying goods, and African music.[80]

African-inspired objects of daily life at Mose have not been preserved in the ground for archaeologists. However, African culture probably influenced the town's crafts, dress, folklore, religion, adornment, music, dance, and ways of farming. This was true of all parts of the Americas where Africans settled, from the slave communities of the United States to the European colonies in the Caribbean and Latin America.

An eighteenth century engraving, Musical Instruments of the African Negroes, *shows African-derived instruments used in Surinam.*[81]

American Indian culture also influenced life at Mose. Some of the men of Mose married Indian women, and others continued to hunt, scout and trade with Indian allies. Like the Spaniards in St. Augustine, the people at Mose adopted local Indian traditions, such as using Indian pottery for a wide variety of everyday activities.

Indian pottery is the most common ceramic type found both at Mose and in the Spanish sites of St. Augustine. Indian potters sometimes made their wares in the shape of European vessels, called "colono-wares". But at Mose, as well as in St. Augustine, traditional Indian vessel forms were usually used by Indians, Africans and Spaniards.[83]

Africans celebrating Carnaval in Rio de Janeiro, Brazil, playing distinctively African instruments.[82]

Indian pot made in the shape of a European pitcher.[84]

HOME AND FAMILY

Archaeology combined with historical documents has given us a glimpse into the home and family life of the people at Mose.

There are no known images of what the people at Mose looked like. Many were first-generation Africans, and may have had such African ornamental features as decorative facial or body scars and filed teeth. They had lived, however, with the English, the Spanish, and sometimes the Indians since they left Africa, and their clothing was probably much like that of the other St. Augustine colonists.

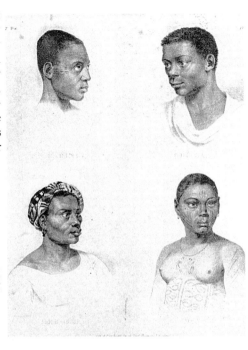

Different African ethnic groups in Brazil, showing ornamental scarification.[85]

Most of the people at Mose lived in small, palm-thatch huts that were described as "resembling those of Indians." Archaeological evidence indicates that at least some of the buildings were oval in shape, and about 12 feet in diameter. They may have been similar to African houses already familiar to the Mose residents. In 1759 there were 22 of these thatch huts at Mose, housing 67 people: 37 men, 15 women, 7 boys, and 8 girls.

A Florida Timucuan Indian village drawn in 1591, showing round houses of palm thatch.[87]

Some clothing items, such as this buckle fragment from Fort Mose, would have been obtained from supplies in St. Augustine. Other items would have been made locally, like bone buttons stamped from long sections of animal bone. Thimbles and pins from Mose indicate the making and mending of clothing.[86]

A West African town in 1732, showing round thatch houses.[88]

The Prospect of the Negroes Town of Rufisco.

The bits and pieces of everyday life recovered by archaeologists at Mose show that life there was filled with attending to the basic necessities: food, shelter, clothing, and defense. There is little to suggest luxury or frivolity.

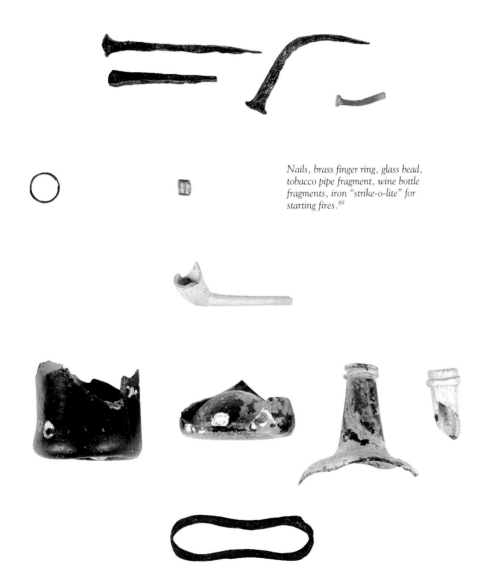

Nails, brass finger ring, glass bead, tobacco pipe fragment, wine bottle fragments, iron "strike-o-lite" for starting fires.[89]

THE MOSE FAMILY TREE

Historian Jane Landers, working with the unusually rich array of historical documents about Mose, has been able to piece together the families who lived at Mose. The religious records alone record births, ethnic origins, naming patterns, godparent networks, deaths, records of epidemics and warfare, and marriages. From these and other sources such as census, legal, and military records we have learned the names of the people, as well as the numbers of men, women and children living at Mose. Sometimes the records stated which African nation a person was from. Most households were typical nuclear families of parents and children, but some all-male households were present as well.

Marriages were often interracial. The African refugees from South Carolina married one another, as well as both free and slave black natives of St. Augustine. Some married Indians, and others married whites. Intermarriage among red, black and white people was common throughout the Spanish New World, and elaborate systems of racial classification were developed, based on the proportions of African, European and American Indian blood a person had. Children were given the mother's legal status, either free or slave. If a Mose militia member married a slave, the wife would have stayed in St. Augustine, along with any children they may have had.

1744 marriage of Juan Fernández, a free black of the Caravali nation, to Flora de la Torre, a Congo slave.[90]

1738 baptism of Calisto, son of a free black father and an Indian mother.[91]

33

Mose was intended to be a farming as well as a defensive community.

The Spaniards in St. Augustine hoped that the Mose farmers could produce enough food not only for themselves, but also as extra food for the colony. They probably farmed corn and maybe rice, but it is clear from the documents that they were unable to meet even their own needs.

The Mose residents supplemented their crops in a number of ways. Residents received government supplies at irregular intervals, including corn, beef, pork, rice, and "biscuit." They also earned extra government food rations by working on government construction projects. Perhaps most importantly, people at Mose hunted and fished in the nearby woods and streams, and probably gathered wild plants and fruits.

Cattle was an important food source for the Spanish colony, and many of the black residents of St. Augustine worked as cowboys.

Most of the black and white residents of eighteenth century St. Augustine were soldiers and soldiers' families. Some Africans also worked to hunt and capture wild horses and cattle remaining in Florida from the previous century. Huge cattle ranches had existed in seventeenth century Florida, until English raids destroyed them.

Africans formed part of the labor force on the seventeenth century ranches, as well as on later eighteenth century ranches.

One of the few cattle ranches that survived into the eighteenth century was that of Diego de Espinosa, located north of St. Augustine. Espinosa was a mulatto who fortified his isolated ranch, which came to be known as "Fort Diego." From it he provided cattle for the town.

Hatched lines indicate the general areas where numerous Spanish cattle ranches thrived during the late seventeenth century.

Horses were used at Mose for transportation, frontier scouting and working the colony's cattle herds. Several buckles found at Fort Mose may have been used on horse tackle. This stirrup, from another St. Augustine site, is similar to those probably used at Mose.[93]

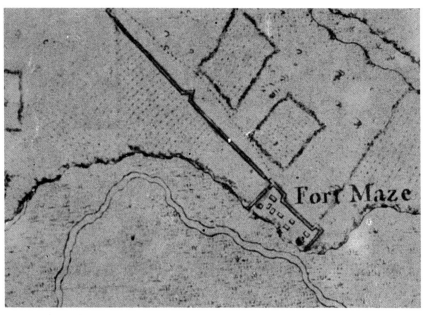

A map of the fort (here called "Fort Maze") showing the nearby agricultural fields.[92]

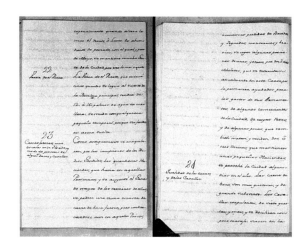

Spanish document from 1759 describing mulattos rounding up wild cattle and horses.[94]

CATHOLIC CONVERTS

One of the conditions for freedom was that all runaway slaves convert to Catholicism.

All of the inhabitants of Mose were Catholic, and received instruction in that faith. There was a church in the town, made of boards and thatch, and a resident missionary priest. The people of Mose were baptized, married, and buried in St. Augustine, however, where the cathedral was located. A few objects that may have been related to religious life were excavated at the fort site.

Possible rosary bead; blue seed beads that may have been used to ward off the evil eye, a North African practice; chain link rosary fragment.[96]

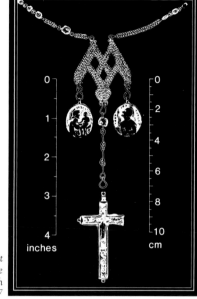

This detail from a sixteenth century map of St. Augustine shows a board and thatch church similar to that built at Mose.[95]

Handmade St. Christopher medallion found at Fort Mose. St. Christopher was the patron saint of Havana and of travelers.[98]

The intricately woven metal links found at Mose may have been from a rosary like this one, excavated from an eighteenth century black cemetery in New Orleans.[97]

Africans were introduced to Catholicism during early Iberian exploration and colonization. A Congo king first adopted Catholicism in 1491, and the tradition was maintained by later kings such as this one shown receiving missionaries in 1648.[99]

The people of Mose probably also formed and joined "cofradias." These were religious and social brotherhoods that were active throughout Spanish America. Their faith may also have blended elements of Catholicism with elements of their traditional African religions, as this was a common practice in other African communities in the Americas.

African gods continue to be worshipped in many areas of the Americas, particularly those influenced by Yoruba culture. These twentieth century images from Brazil evoke the spirit of this Yoruba-derived religious tradition. Gods shown are (left to right): Nana Buruku, Ossiam, Exu, Iansa, Ogun and Xango (below). [101]

A Brazilian church scene where a black brotherhood performs religious rituals that blend African and European traditions. [100]

These dance wands show the amazing continuity between Africa (Yoruba culture) and the Americas (Brazilian Candomble) in certain religious practices. In spite of slight name changes and variations in iconography, the core beliefs and ritual materials remain the same. Shango, the powerful god of thunder and lightning, is associated with a double-headed axe. (left - African Shango Wand; right - Brazilian Xango Wand) [102]

ABANDONMENT AND DECLINE

The second Fort Mose was occupied by the black community for eleven years.

Ten years after its establishment, the Fort Mose fortification was strengthened by an earthwork and moat that extended some two miles west to the San Sebastian River. This earthwork served to strengthen the northernmost fortified defense line protecting St. Augustine from the English. Ironically, Florida became an English colony the very next year. In 1763, the war known as the French and Indian war in the Americas, and as the Seven Years War in Europe, ended. The Treaty of Paris gave Florida to England, and Cuba back to Spain.

Mose was abandoned as an African-American community in 1763, when Florida became an English colony.

All of the inhabitants of the Spanish colony left their homes and sailed to Cuba, including the people of Mose, and the eighty-six Indians who lived in St. Augustine. Some of the Mose residents settled in the Matanzas province. Once in Cuba, they again had to start a new life in an unfamiliar land.

Fort Mose was refurbished by the English, and was used as a fort during their twenty-year occupation of Florida. When the Spaniards returned in 1784, they too used Mose as a military outpost. It was finally destroyed and abandoned in 1812. In that year, the fort was occupied by a group of American adventurers (known as the "Florida Patriots"), who intended to capture Florida for the United States. They failed, and the fort was destroyed for the last time by the Spanish, African, and Indian troops who routed the Patriots. It gradually fell into ruin until its rediscovery more than a century later.

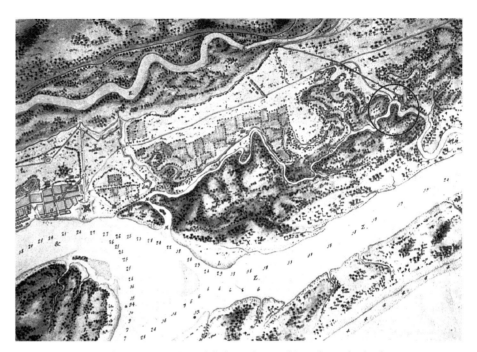

This 1791 map shows Fort Mose (encircled) during the second Spanish period, after the twenty year English occupation of Florida, and shortly before it was destroyed forever.[103]

Map of Cuba, showing the Matanzas province where St. Augustine residents settled.

Today's view of the island where Fort Mose is buried.

THE SEARCH FOR A LOST FORT

For more than 150 years after its abandonment Fort Mose was buried from history on a remote island in the Florida marsh. It has required the combined efforts of many different scientists, historians, and legislators to rediscover Mose and bring to light a long-lost and little-known chapter of our colonial past.

The owner of the Fort Mose site, Mr. Jack Williams of St. Augustine, had long suspected that the fort was on his property, and invited archaeologists to study the site. The Florida Legislature, encouraged by Representative Bill Clark and the Black Legislative Caucus, recognized the importance of the Fort Mose site and lent its support to an ongoing research project. Led by Dr. Kathleen Deagan of the Florida Museum of Natural History at the University of Florida, a team of historians, archaeologists, and other specialists has uncovered an impressive range of detail about the fort, its inhabitants, and their everyday life.

Aerial view of the Fort Mose site (the island in the foreground).

Much of what we know about the fort comes from centuries-old documents and maps in the colonial archives of Spain, Florida, Cuba, and South Carolina. Dr. Jane Landers, historian at Vanderbilt University, has worked extensively with these documents. A variety of maps showed the fort, and other documents added information about the fort and people in the community.

Historical documents were combined with space age technology to determine the location of Fort Mose. The first fort, built in 1738 and destroyed two years later during Oglethorpe's siege on St. Augustine, is today inundated by a salt marsh. Although its underwater location has prevented excavation, "thermal" images taken by a branch of NASA helped to reveal the small square structure.

Jane Landers working with microfilmed documents.

Old Spanish and English documents provided a wealth of information about Fort Mose.[104]

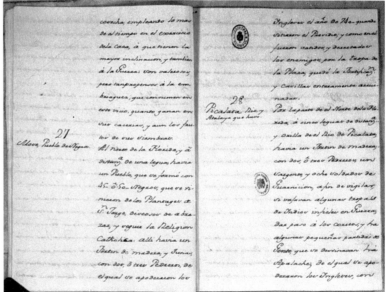

Former land owner Jack Williams, archaeologist Kathleen Deagan, and Florida State Representative Bill Clark, standing in front of the Fort Mose site.

Thermal Clues to Fort Mose

Using technology developed by NASA as part of the space program, images such as this one were generated for the Fort Mose site area. Although it looks like a photograph, it is actually a computer-generated image which tells us how much heat is held by different parts of the ground. More heat is often retained in areas that people have altered (such as moats and roads).

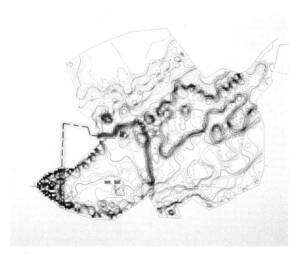

Thermal imagery is the best clue to the possible location of the first Fort Mose. Archaeologists believe that this image reveals the outline of the original fort, twenty meters to a side (circled).

The second Fort Mose, built in 1752 and abandoned in 1763, was rediscovered by a combined study of aerial photographs, old maps, and archaeological remains. First, modern aerial photos and eighteenth century maps were printed at the same scale. When they were overlaid, the fort fell on what is today a small island in the marsh.

Archaeologists then began to study the island. They created a contour map of the site, which shows slight rises and depressions in the ground that cannot be seen by the eye alone. Such differences in elevation often show where past human activity took place. The

contour map showed clearly where the walls of the fort had been. It also showed that one corner of the fort had been destroyed by a tidal creek. Archaeologists used the contour map in conjunction with historic maps of the site to guide their excavations.

Overlay of modern aerial photo with the 1763 Castello map.

Contour map of the Fort Mose site, with an outline of the fort.

Map of the Fort Mose site, showing areas excavated by archaeologists.

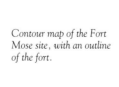

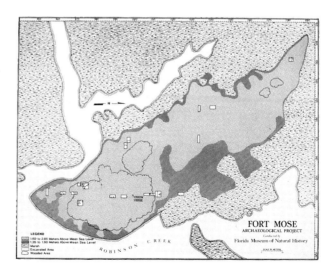

Excavations revealed the fort's moat, remnants of the clay-faced earthwork, and traces of post and footing supports for interior buildings.

An excavation unit at Fort Mose. Excavation proceeds by hand very slowly, removing no more than 2 inches of dirt at a time.

Mapping soil patterns is a regular part of the excavation process, providing "pictures" of how the site is put together.

Keeping records of the excavation and the exact location of everything found requires more work than the actual digging itself. This is the most important part of the archaeological process for correctly interpreting the findings.

All soil is screened through different mesh screens down to 1/16 of an inch in size, in order to capture the smallest artifact fragments, plant remains and animal bones.

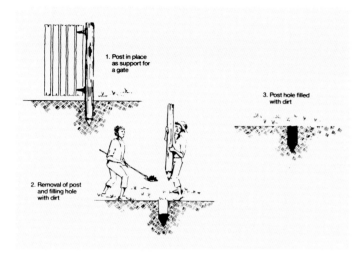

1. Post in place as support for a gate

2. Removal of post and filling hole with dirt

3. Post hole filled with dirt

Side view of part of the moat. Note the dark soil with shells, which dips down to the left toward the base of the moat.

At the back of this photograph is the top view of part of the moat, identified by a large band of dark soil.

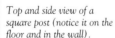

Top and side view of a square post (notice it on the floor and in the wall).

Physical evidence of the fort is difficult to see with the untrained eye. These photographs show the soil stains that are the only remains of the moat (now filled with soil), the wooden posts used in construction, and the wooden footings used to support buildings.

The artifacts from Fort Mose have provided detail about daily life at the fort, from diet to building construction. By combining all sources of information, from the archives of Spain to the soils of the former fort, researchers are reconstructing a social history for the people at Fort Mose, more than two hundred years ago.

Top view of one large round post (background) and a long building footing (foreground).

Artifacts as they are recovered during screening at Fort Mose.

41

A THIN SLICE OF TIME

The most valuable information in an archaeological site is the soil itself - patterns in color, texture and formation that indicate past human activity.

This is a replica of an actual excavation unit at Fort Mose. In this unit, archaeologists uncovered the remains of the fort moat (B), evidence of the clay facing on the fort's earthen walls (C), and a hole dug for a wooden post which may have been used to strengthen the fort wall (D,E). These are evident to archaeologists as distinctive soil stains.

Soil profiles such as this one show that the occupation of the site spanned thousands of years, beginning with an early Indian occupation and ending in the twentieth century. The black fort was only a brief episode of the site history, represented by just 10-20 centimeters of soil. Great care was taken during excavation to insure that no information was lost from the thin layer that represents the African-American settlement of Fort Mose.

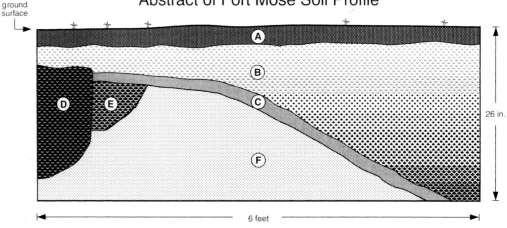

Abstract of Fort Mose Soil Profile

ground surface

26 in.

6 feet

Key to soil profile drawing
A = Modern topsoil
B = Soil used to fill in the moat and level the site, possibly for expansion of the fort during the Second Spanish Period in the 1790's. Upper portion of this deposit also contains materials accumulated during later use of the site.
C = Layer of clay which may have been used to face the fort's earthen walls, and which later slumped into the moat.
D = Evidence of a large wooden post which was probably used in construction of the fort wall. After the post was removed or disintegrated, its shape was retained by the dark gray-brown soil which replaced it.
E = Part of the hole which was dug to sink the large wooden post in the ground. After the post was in place, the rest of the hole was filled with dense, packed shells to stabilize the post.
F = Pre-fort soils with evidence of Indian occupation. Indian populations used the site for thousands of years, ranging from the Timucuan Indians who lived in the area when Europeans first arrived, to the Archaic period as long ago as 6500 B.C.

Replica excavation unit, Fort Mose exhibit

The diet of the Mose residents has been reconstructed by zooarchaeologists and archaeobotanists, specialists who study food remains from archaeological sites.

Screening of soil through very fine mesh allows archaeologists to find tiny bones and seeds in the garbage of the people who once lived on a site. Dirt is also "floated," or separated with water, so that light plant and animal remains float to the top and heavy dirt particles sink.

A crew member "floating" the soil through fine screens.

An unsorted sample of plant remains from Mose, separated from the soil during the flotation process.

Sorting the tiny fragments of bone and shell from the 1/16 inch screen sample.

The zooarchaeologists identify the bones, the archaeobotanists identify the plants and seeds, and the field archaeologist identifies food preparation artifacts and methods. From this evidence they can usually reconstruct what people were eating in the past, what plants were growing in the area, and other unrecorded bits of information for understanding past lifeways.

Zooarchaeologist Elizabeth Reitz identified thousands of shells and bones from Mose.

Archaeobotanist Margaret Scarry spent many hours doing precise sorting under a microscope to identify tiny plant remains and wood species used at the site.

Specialists studying the animal bones from Mose have found that the people ate mostly locally available, wild foods, such as the fish, shellfish, turtles, rabbits, deer, and other animals that could be found near the village.

Although the remains of plants were not well preserved in the soils of Mose, we can assume that the people took advantage of wild and domesticated plants used by other St. Augustine residents. These included oranges, figs, nuts, squashes, gourds, melons, beans, huckleberries, plums, persimmons, blueberries, blackberries, maypop and grapes.

Objects used in the preparation and consumption of food, such as corn grinding stones, cooking pots, spoons and storage jars, were excavated from Mose. These items also help reconstruct what foods were used and how they were prepared.

Artifacts related to food storage and preparation found at Fort Mose, left to right: sherds from Spanish olive jars used to ship and store food; sherds from Indian cooking pots; part of a stone mano used to grind grains (note the flat surface); spoon handle.[105]

Artifacts and other material remains from Fort Mose tell us a great deal about the lives of the people who lived there.

Hundreds of artifacts were recovered during excavations at Fort Mose. Most of these were broken fragments no larger than a thumbnail. In spite of their size, these artifacts have often been the only clues to daily activity at the fort - cooking and eating, house construction, defense, religion, and entertainment.

By knowing the exact position of each fragment in the earth, archaeologists can also tell when and where the activities represented by these artifacts occurred. This is the kind of information that does not appear in written history, and that archaeology alone can provide.

Once excavated and recorded, artifacts are studied and treated in the laboratory. Ultimately, all of the information about the artifacts is combined with the information from the excavations and the analyses of the historians, zooarchaeologists, archaeobotanists, and a report is written. The information is also used in preparing museum exhibits.

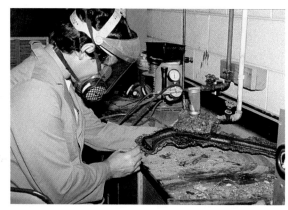

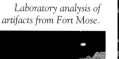

Many of the artifacts required specialized treatment and conservation to prevent decay and insure their survival. This was done by an archaeological conservator. Conservator James Levy, who worked on the Fort Mose metals, is seen here using conservation techniques to clean a gun from another Florida site.

Fort Mose exhibit.

Laboratory analysis of artifacts from Fort Mose.

EPILOGUE

Fort Mose stands as a monument to the courageous African Americans who risked, and often lost, their lives in the long struggle to achieve freedom.

Their legacy is one of tremendous daring and effort, and one which made important contributions to our colonial past. It is critical to our understanding of history that we recognize that the African experience in colonial history was much more than slavery and oppression. Fort Mose is one example of the many reactions against slavery. Its story helps to create a broader vision of our American heritage.

The Fort Mose site is the only site of its kind in the United States, and is a precious and vulnerable part of our state and national patrimony. The Florida Legislature recognized the significance of the site and approved its purchase. It is now under the jurisdiction of the Florida Department of Environmental Protection, and will soon be recognized as a National Historic Landmark. Fort Mose will ultimately serve to interpret and communicate the story of this early fortress of freedom.

ILLUSTRATION REFERENCES

[1]Naval battle between England and Spain, Venezuela, 1743; Archivo Generál de Indias, Seville.

[2]Detail from Cresques map, ca. 1375; Bibliothèque National, Paris.

[3]Olfert Dapper, *Description de l'Afrique* (Amsterdam: Wolfgang, Waesberge, Boom & Van Someren, 1686).

[4]John Barbot, *A Description of the Coasts of North and South Guinea; and of Ethiopia Inferior, vulgarly Angola*. In Awnsham Churchhill, *A Collection of Voyages and Travel* (London: J. Walthoe, 1732).

[5]William Allen, *A Narrative of the Expedition to the River Niger in 1841* (London: R. Bentley, 1848).

[6]John Barbot, *A Description of the Coasts of North and South Guinea; and of Ethiopia Inferior, vulgarly Angola*. In Awnsham Churchhill, *A Collection of Voyages and Travels* (London: J. Walthoe, 1732).

[7]Anonymous French engraving, 17th century; Biblothèque National, Paris.

[8]Congo mask. Harn Museum of Art, Gainesville, Florida; S-72-25.

[9]Ijaw altar piece. Rodney McGalliard collection.

[10]Mande tunic. William Arnett collection.

[11]Isabela Polychrome plate fragment, La Isabela, Dominican Republic; Florida Museum of Natural History, Gainesville, HTC. Stirrup base, La Vega Vieja, Dominican Republic; Florida Museum of Natural History, HTC. Cuenca Tile, Convento de San Francisco, Florida; Florida Museum of Natural History, HTC/A-11172. Moorish style glass vial, Panamá Viejo; Florida Museum of Natural History, HTC/CL-12. Book clasp, Puerto Real, Haiti; Florida Museum of Natural History, PR85-3301. Key hole cover, Puerto Real, Haiti; Florida Museum of Natural History, PR81-1861.

[12]*Cantigas of Alfonso X*, 13th century; El Escorial, Madrid.

[13]*Cantigas of Alfonso X*, 13th century; El Escorial, Madrid.

[14]*Chessbook of Alfonso X*, 1283; El Escorial, Madrid.

[15]*Chessbook of Alfonso X*, 1283; El Escorial, Madrid.

[16]Courtesy Rare Books Library, University of Florida.

[17]*Fueros del Reino de Aragon* (Barcelona, ca. 1260-80).

[18]Anonymous German image, 1525-27; Hofbibliothek, Aschaffenburg, Germany.

[19]Baltasar Teles, *História da Etiopía A Alta*, 1660. Biblioteca Nacional de Lisboa, Portugal.

[20]Rijksmuseum Nederlands Scheepvaart Museum, Amsterdam.

[21]John Barbot, *A Description of the Coasts of North and South Guinea; and of Ethiopia Inferior, vulgarly Angola*. In Awnsham Churchhill, *A Collection of Voyages and Travels* (London: J. Walthoe, 1732).

[22]Drawing by Michael Falck, Florida Museum of Natural History, Gainesville.

[23]Illustration for Columbus' letter to the King; Giuliano Dati, *The First Letter of Columbus* (Florence, 1495).

[24]Theodore deBry, *America* (Frankfurt, 1596).

[25]Theodore deBry, *America* (Frankfurt, 1596).

[26]En Bas Saline, Haiti; Florida Museum of Natural History, Gainesville; Adornos: EBS-88-7192, EBS-86-3808, EBS-88-6918, EBS-88-7012, EBS-84-3897, EBS-85-6321; Celts: EBS-85-6779, EBS-86-6833; Stamp: EBS-84-4017; Beads: EBS-85-5867, EBS-87-6892, EBS-85-6434, EBS-85-6649, EBS-88-7321, EBS-85-4645, EBS-85-4474; Zemi: EBS-88-7273.

[27]Florida Museum of Natural History, Gainesville; PR-3175-19-27, PR-3151-19-28, PR-3204-19-5.

[28]From Jerald T. Milanich and Susan Milbrath, editors, *First Encounters* (Gainesville: University of Florida Press, 1989).

[29]William Hodges, Haiti.

[30]Fray Bernardino de Sahagún, *Florentine Codex*, or *História General de las Cosas de Nueva España* (Santa Fe: School of American Research, 1900; orig. ca. 1568).

[31]Aquarelas Carybe, *Iconografia dos Deuses Africanos no Candomble da Bahia* (Brazil, 1980); courtesy Charles Fox.

[32]Harn Museum of Art, Gainesville, Florida.

[33]Cesar de Rochefort, *Histoire Naturelle des Iles Antilles* (Rotterdam: R. Leers, 1681).

[34]Fray Diego Durán, *História de las Indias de Nueva España y Islas de Tierra Firme* (Mexico: Editora Nacionál, 1951; orig. 1581).

[35]Drawing by Michael Falck, Florida Museum of Natural History, Gainesville.

[36]Theodore deBry, *America* (Frankfurt, 1596).

[37]John Gabriel Stedman, *Narrative of a Five Years Expedition Against the Revolted Negroes of Surinam, 1772 to 1777* (London: J. Johnson, 1796).

[38]National Library, Kingston, Jamaica.

[39]Museo de las Américas, Madrid.

[40]Collección de la Fundación García Arévalo, Santo Domingo.

[41]Phelipe Guaman Poma de Ayala, *Primer Nueva Coronica y Buen Gobierno*; early 17th century; Royal Library, Copenhagen.

[42]Museo Nacionál de História, Mexico City.

[43]Thomas Clarkson, *History of the Rise, Progress and Accomplishment of the Abolition of the African Slave Trade*, 1806; Courtesy Library Company of Philadelphia.

[44]A.M. French, *Slavery in South Carolina* (New York: W.M. French, 1862); Library of Congress.

[45]Florida Bureau of Archaeological Research, Tallahassee; L06814, L06819, 2324/73, L06817 & 2436/73, 2432/73.

[46]Alice Huger Smith, "Planting rice in the African manner," in Elizabeth W.A. Pringle, *A Woman Rice Planter* (New York: Macmillan Company, 1913).

[47]Joachim Monteiro, *Angola and the River Congo* (London: Macmillan, 1875).

[48]Alice Huger Smith in Elizabeth W.A. Pringle, *A Woman Rice Planter* (New York: Macmillan Company, 1913).

[49]Drawing by Michael Falck, Florida Museum of Natural History, Gainesville.

[50]Courtesy P.K. Yonge Library of Florida History, Gainesville, AGI SD 58-1-2/74, Nov. 7, 1693.

[51]Thomas Branagan, *The Penitential Tyrant* (Philadelphia, 1805).

[52]Courtesy P.K. Yonge Library of Florida History, Gainesville.

[53-54]Pupo - James Moncrief, 1765; Picolata - Pedro Ruiz de Olano, 1738; P.K. Yonge

Library of Florida History, Gainesville.

[55]Courtesy P.K. Yonge Library of Florida History, Gainesville.

[56]F.E. Williams collection.

[57]Joachim Monteiro, *Angola and the River Congo* (London: Macmillan, 1875).

[58]Pablo Castello, 1763; Courtesy St. Augustine Historical Society.

[59]Drawing based upon research by historians Albert Manucy and Luis Arana.

[60]Courtesy P.K. Yonge Library of Florida History; Gainesville; Father Juan Joseph de Solana to Bishop Pedro Agustín Morél de Sanchez, April 22, 1759, SD 516, microfilm reel 28K.

[61]Courtesy P.K. Yonge Library of Florida History; Gainesville; Report by Captain of Artillery, Don Manuel de Barros, 4/20/1759, AGI SD 2604.

[62]Museo Romántico, Madrid.

[63]Flintlock Musket barrel, lock, butt stock, butt plate (1700 and 1733 shipwrecks; Florida Bureau of Archaeological Research,Tallahassee, L3872, L6004, L2041, L06818); Socket Bayonet for Musket (ca. 1760, Fort Gadsden, Florida; Florida Bureau of Archaeological Research, L4735); Wooden Ramrod and Brass Holder (Ramrod: 1715 shipwreck Florida Bureau of Archaeological Research, L06816; Holder: Historic St. Augustine Preservation Board, MTC, Plaza Well 2 FS 10); Ramrod Tip (Historic St. Augustine Preservation Board, SA 16-23).

[64]Spanish Plate fleet shipwreck, ca. 1715; Florida Bureau of Archaeological Research, Tallahassee, L06815, 437.

[65]Nozzle - Florida Bureau of Archaeological Research, Tallahassee, 79.60.00.178-180; balls and flints - Fort Mose, Florida Museum of Natural History, balls: 87-45-1000 (2), 87-45-1055; flints: 87-45-1000, -1118, -1435.

[66]Vita Bonfadini, *La Caccia Dell'Arcobugio* (Italy, 1691).

[67]Joseph Hefter, in *Artes de México*, No.102, 1968.

[68]Archivo General de Indias, Seville.

[69]Original source unknown; appears in Ferran Soldevila, *História de España*, vol. 5 (Barcelona: Ariel, 1964).

[70]*Procession of the Viceroy*, detail, Museo Nacionál de História, Chapultepec Castle, Mexico City.

[71]Archivo General de Indias, Seville.

[72]Archivo General de Simancas, M.P. y D. XVI-136. S.G., Leg. 7255.

[73]Archivo General de Simancas, M.P. y D. XLVII-56 & 57. S.G., Leg. 6850.

[74]Arquivo Histórico Coloniál, Brazil.

[75]Archivo Generál de Indias, Seville.

[76]Archivo Generál de Simancas.

[77]Anonymous 18th century engraving; Bibliothèque National, Paris.

[78]Courtesy P.K. Yonge Library of Florida History, Gainesville; AGI SD 2658, 87-3-12.

[79]Agostino Brunias, *Scene with Dancing in the West Indies*, ca. 1770-80; present whereabouts unknown; appears in Pierre Pluchon, *Histoire des Antilles et de la Guyane* (Toulouse, 1982).

[80]Jean Baptiste Debret, *Voyage Pittoresque et Historique au Brésil* (Paris: Firmin Didot Freres, 1834-1839).

[81]John Gabriel Stedman, *Narrative of a Five Years Expedition Against the Revolted Slaves of Surinam* (London: J. Johnson, 1796).

[82]Jean Baptiste Debret, *Voyage Pittoresque et Historique au Brésil* (Paris: Firmin Didot Freres, 1834-1839).

[83]Florida Museum of Natural History, Gainesville, Tatham Mound, 88-19-350.

[84]Santa Catalina de Guale mission, Florida Archeological Services.

[85]Johann Moritz Rugendas, *Voyage Pittoresque dans le Brésil* (Paris, 1835).

[86]Florida Museum of Natural History, Gainesville; buckle: 87-45-1000; bone button: 89-2-1015, SA42A-754; thimble: 71-51-A3609; pins: 87-45-1529, -1545.

[87]Theodore deBry, *America* (Frankfurt, 1596).

[88]John Barbot, *A Description of the Coasts of North and South Guinea; and of Ethiopia Inferior, vulgarly Angola*. In Awnsham Churchhill, *A Collection of Voyages and Travels* (London: J. Walthoe, 1732).

[89]Florida Museum of Natural History, Gainesville; Fort Mose, nails: 87-45-1000, -1001 (2), -1005; ring: 87-45-1391; bead: 87-45-1547; pipe: 87-45-1442; bottles: 87-45-surface, -1207, -1414, -1005; strike-o-lite: 71-51-A3606.

[90]Courtesy P.K. Yonge Library of Florida History, Gainesville; St. Augustine Cathedral Parish Records, microfilm reel 284C.

[91]Courtesy P.K. Yonge Library of Florida History, Gainesville; St. Augustine Cathedral Parish Records, Black Baptisms, microfilm reel 284F.

[92]ca. 1752; Courtesy St. Augustine Historical Society.

[93]Buckle: Florida Museum of Natural History,Gainesville, 71-51-A3607; stirrup: Historic St. Augustine Preservation Board, MTC.

[94]Courtesy P.K. Yonge Library of Florida History, Gainesville; Griñan report, microfilm reel 141P, ms. 11265.19.

[95]Line fascimile from *Mapa del Pueblo*, ca. 1593; courtesy Albert Manucy, *The Houses of St. Augustine* (St. Augustine Historical Society, 1978).

[96]Florida Museum of Natural History, Gainesville; bead: 87-45-1307; seed beads: 87-45-1232, -1347; rosary: 71-51-A3598.

[97]Louisiana State University.

[98]F. E. Williams collection.

[99]Giovanni Antonio Cavazzi, *Istorica Descrittione de Tre Regni Congo, Matamba, et Angola* (Bologna: Monti, 1687).

[100]Jean Baptiste Debret, study for book *Voyage Pittoresque et Historique au Brésil*, 1826; Museus Raymundo Ottoni de Castro Maya, Rio de Janeiro.

[101]Nelson B. Faedrich, 1978; courtesy Charles Fox.

[102]Florida Museum of Natural History, E-248; Charles Fox collection.

[103]Mariano de la Rocque; Courtesy St. Augustine Historical Society.

[104]Courtesy P.K. Yonge Library of Florida History, Gainesville; Griñan report, reel 141P, ms. 11265.19.

[105]Florida Museum of Natural History, Gainesville; olive jar: 87-45-1118, -1354, -1307; Indian: 87-45-1520, -1588, 71-51-A3608; mano: 87-45-1236.

FURTHER READING

Arana, Luis
  1973   The Mose site. *El Escribano* Vol. 10:50-62. St. Augustine
          Historical Society.

Camp, Betty Dunckel
  1990   Fort Mose Educational Packet. Gainesville: Florida Museum
          of Natural History.

Carroll, Patrick J.
  1991   *Blacks in Colonial Vera Cruz: Race, Ethnicity, and Regional Development.*
          Austin: University of Texas Press.

Deagan, Kathleen
  1983   *Spanish St. Augustine: The Archaeology of a Colonial Creole
          Community.* New York: Academic Press.

  1991   *America's Ancient City: Spanish St. Augustine 1565-1763.*
          Volume 25 in *Spanish Borderlands Sourcebooks*, edited by David
          Hurst Thomas. New York: Garland.

Ferguson, Leland
  1992   *Uncommon Ground: Archaeology and Early African America,
          1650-1800.* Washington, D.C.: Smithsonian Institution Press.

Hall, Gwendolyn Midlo
  1992   *Africans in Colonial Louisiana: The Development of Afro-Creole
          Culture in the Eighteenth Century.* Baton Rouge: Louisiana State
          University Press.

Henderson, Ann L., and Gary Mormino, editors
  1991   *Spanish Pathways in Florida.* Sarasota: Pineapple Press.

Landers, Jane
  1984   Spanish Sanctuary: Fugitives in Florida 1687-1790. *The
          Florida Historical Quarterly* 62(3):296-313.

  1990a   Gracia Real de Santa Teresa de Mose: A Free Black Town in
          Spanish Colonial Florida. *The American Historical Review*
          95(1):9-30.

  1990b   African Presence in Early Spanish Colonization of the
          Caribbean and the Southeastern Borderlands. In *Columbian
          Consequences, Volume II: Archaeological and Historical Perspectives
          on the Spanish Borderlands East*, edited by David Hurst Thomas.
          Washington, D.C.: Smithsonian Institution Press, pp. 315-327.

Mullin, Michael
  1992   *Africa and America; Slave Acculturation and Resistance in the
          American South and the British Caribbean, 1736-1831.* Urbana:
          University of Illinois Press.

Mulroy, Kevin
  1993   *Freedom on the Border: The Seminole Maroons in Florida, the
          Indian Territory, Coahuila, and Texas.* Lubbock: Texas Tech
          University Press.

Patrick, Rembert, editor
  1949   Letters of the Invaders of East Florida, 1812. *The Florida
          Historical Quarterly* XXVIII, July:53-69.

Price, Richard
  1979   *Maroon Societies: Rebel Slave Communities in the Americas.*
          Baltimore: John Hopkins Press.

Rout, Leslie B., Jr.
  1976   *The African Experience in Spanish America.* Cambridge:
          Cambridge University Press.

South Carolina Archives
  1954   *The St. Augustine Expedition of 1740.* Columbia.

Tepaske, John
  1975   The Fugitive Slave; Inter-Colonial Rivalry and Spanish Slave
          Policy, 1687-1764. In *18th Century Florida and its Borderlands*,
          edited by Samuel Proctor. Gainesville: University Presses of Florida.

Thornton, John
  1992   *Africa and Africans in the Making of the Atlantic World, 1400-
          1680.* Cambridge: Cambridge University Press.

Usner, Daniel H.
  1992   *Indians, Settlers and Slaves in a Frontier Exchange Economy.*
          Chapel Hill: University of North Carolina Press.

Wood, Peter H.
  1974   *Black Majority.* New York: W.W. Norton & Company.

Wright, Irene
  1924   Dispatches of Spanish Officials Bearing on the Free Negro
          Settlement of Gracia Real de Santa Teresa de Mose. *Journal of
          Negro History* 9:144-193.

INDEX

Library of Congress Cataloging-in-Publication Data

Deagan, Kathleen A.
    Fort Mose : colonial America's Black fortress of freedom /
Kathleen Deagan and Darcie MacMahon.
        p.   cm.
    Includes bibliographical references and index.
    ISBN 0-8130-1351-8 (cloth). -- ISBN 0-8130-1352-6 (paper)
    1. Fort Mose Site (Fla.). 2. Afro-Americans--Florida--Antiquities.
3. Afro-Americans--Florida--History--18th century. 4. Fugitive
slaves--Florida--History--18th century. 5. Florida--History--
Spanish colony, 1565-1763. I. MacMahon, Darcie A. II. Title.
F319.F734D43 1995
975.9'18--dc20   94-42953
                                                     CIP